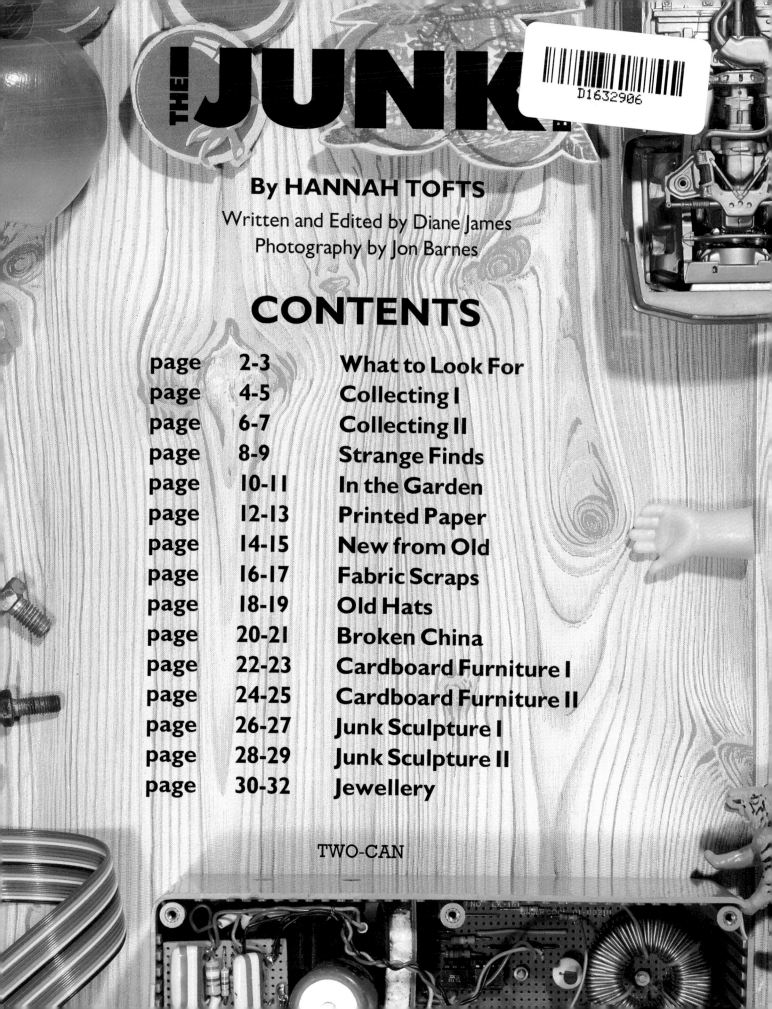

THE JUNK

By **HANNAH TOFTS**

Written and Edited by Diane James

Photography by Jon Barnes

CONTENTS

TWO-CAN

In this book you will find out what we did with things that most people would call junk and probably throw away!

Once you start collecting and making things you will discover that even the oldest, shabbiest things can be made to look interesting. You will not need any special equipment but the following will be useful – craft knife, scissors, glue, paint, stapler and a hole punch. Make sure that anything you use really is junk and will not be needed again!

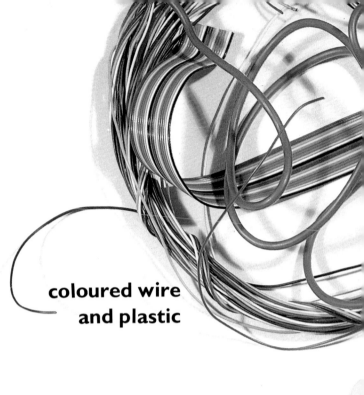

coloured wire and plastic

nuts, bolts, screws and washers

buttons and beads

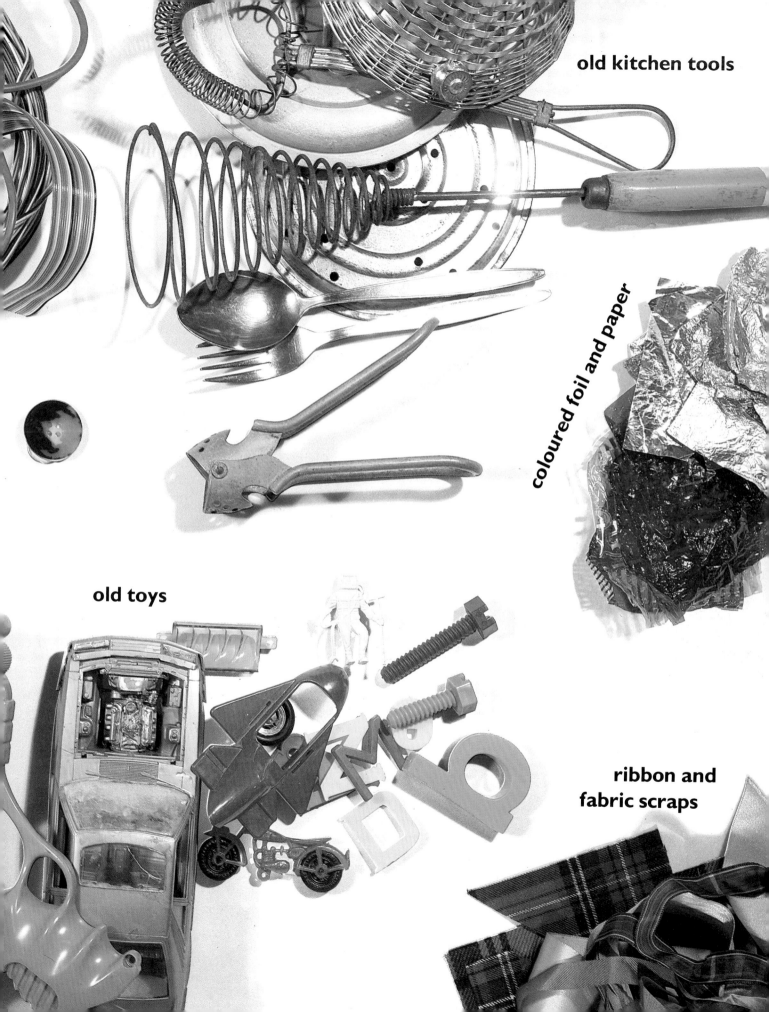

old kitchen tools

coloured foil and paper

old toys

ribbon and
fabric scraps

Making a collection can be good fun and need not be expensive. Choose a theme and make sure all your friends know so they can help too! If you have enough room, try turning your collection into an interesting display like the one here.

The seaside is a perfect place for collecting all sorts of interesting things such as shells, driftwood, pebbles and seaweed. Look in gift shops on the sea front for inexpensive souvenirs to decorate your room.

People throw away the strangest things! With a coat of paint, these abandoned baskets look terrific and they can be used for storing things or displaying a collection.

Why not turn a corner of your room into a garden that will flower all year! Jumble sales are good for plastic flowers and garden centres may have off-cuts of trellis and fencing. Look out for abandoned flower pots and add some real plants for a touch of green.

If your shelves and chest of drawers are looking a bit shabby, give them a new look by covering them with old newspapers and comics. First, use fine sandpaper to smooth the surface of the wood.

Cut or tear the newspaper and comics into pieces, thinking about what colours you want to look strong on the finished object. Glue the paper pieces to the wood surface and don't worry if they overlap.

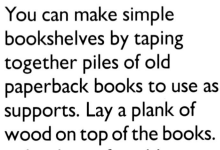

You can make simple bookshelves by taping together piles of old paperback books to use as supports. Lay a plank of wood on top of the books.

Look out for old vases and picture frames to decorate in the same way as your furniture.

Here are some ideas for decorating picture frames. Look out for frames that have been thrown away. Give them a coat of paint and glue on objects such as nuts and bolts, shells, pebbles and dried pasta – or use fabric or paper. Stick your favourite picture in the frame.

Here are some ideas for making albums and books with smart fabric covers.

Cut two pieces of sturdy card for the back and front. Then cut two pieces of fabric to cover the card leaving a turning all the way round to glue under. Spread glue on one side of each piece of card and stick the fabric down. Cut across the corners as in the photograph. Allow an extra few millimetres (the thickness of the card) to make neat corners when you glue the fabric under.

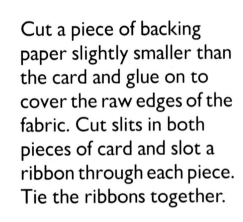

Cut a piece of backing paper slightly smaller than the card and glue on to cover the raw edges of the fabric. Cut slits in both pieces of card and slot a ribbon through each piece. Tie the ribbons together.

Or use a bradawl to punch holes through the card. Slip two key rings through the holes to keep the pieces of card together.

Look out for old battered hats at jumble sales. Go through your junk collection to find things to decorate them with. We used plastic fruit and flowers to make our dramatic hats. You can attach objects with double sided tape or with pieces of thin wire.

The next time someone breaks a cup or saucer, pick up the pieces and put them in a box! You may also find chipped or broken china at jumble sales. When you have a collection of pieces, sort them into colours and put them in jam jars to make a colourful display.

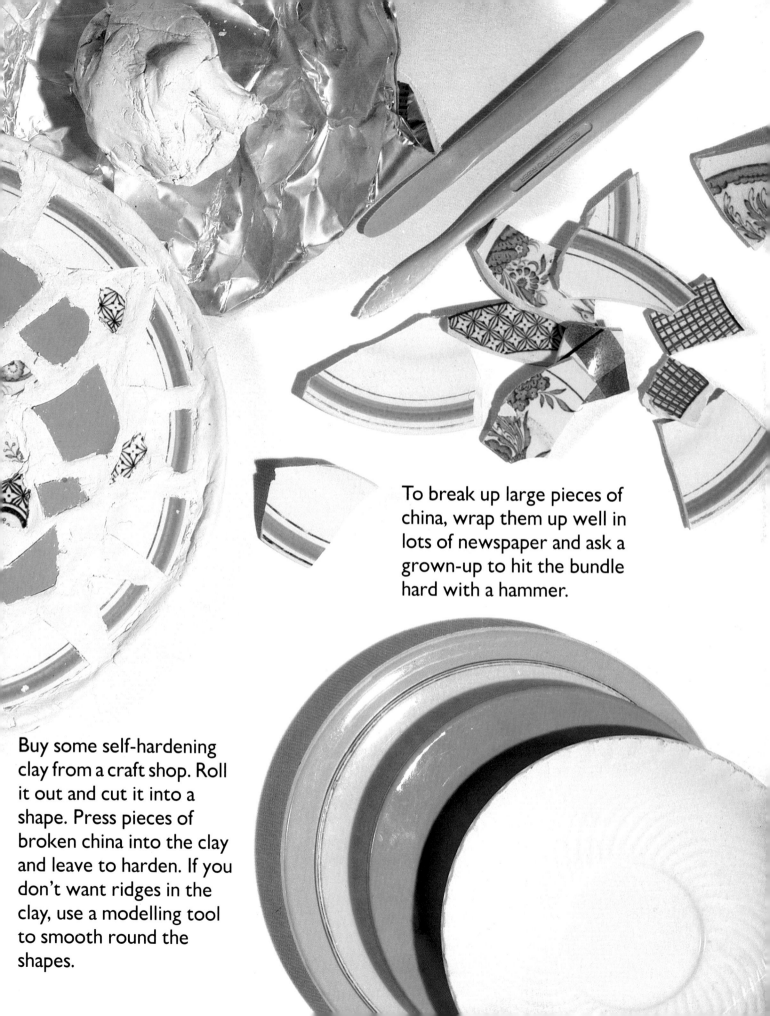

To break up large pieces of china, wrap them up well in lots of newspaper and ask a grown-up to hit the bundle hard with a hammer.

Buy some self-hardening clay from a craft shop. Roll it out and cut it into a shape. Press pieces of broken china into the clay and leave to harden. If you don't want ridges in the clay, use a modelling tool to smooth round the shapes.

Look out for strong cardboard boxes in all shapes and sizes – shops and supermarkets usually have a good supply!

By cutting, gluing, slitting and slotting, you can transform your boxes into designer-style furniture for your room.

Coffee Table

Find a good size cardboard fruit box and cut off the top and bottom, leaving just the four sides. Cut one of the sides down the middle to make supports for the table. Fold the supports in towards the middle, making sure that the sides of the table are at right angles to the top. You may need to add extra pieces of card to make sure that the supports reach the table top. Tape the supports to the underside of the table top as in the photograph. For extra support, tape another piece of card between the supports. Paint the table with vinyl paint.

Slit and Slot Table

Cut out two pieces of card A and B and four pieces of card C that are half the width of A and B. Make slits as in the photograph in each of the pieces of card. The slits should be exactly half the depth of the pieces of card. Slot A over B at X and then slot all the pieces marked C over the pieces marked O. Cut a strong piece of card to go on the top and secure with strong tape. Paint the table with vinyl paint or decorate with collage.

Fruit Box Chair

Find a good size fruit box and cut off the top and the bottom. Cut across the diagonals of two opposite sides as in the photograph. Stick the triangles cut off inside the arms for extra support.

For the base, cut the top off another similar sized box. To strengthen the base, cut two pieces of card the same width and depth as the box, make slits in the middle of each piece using the same method as before and slot them together. Put this structure into the box. Tape the base to the top and paint with vinyl paint.

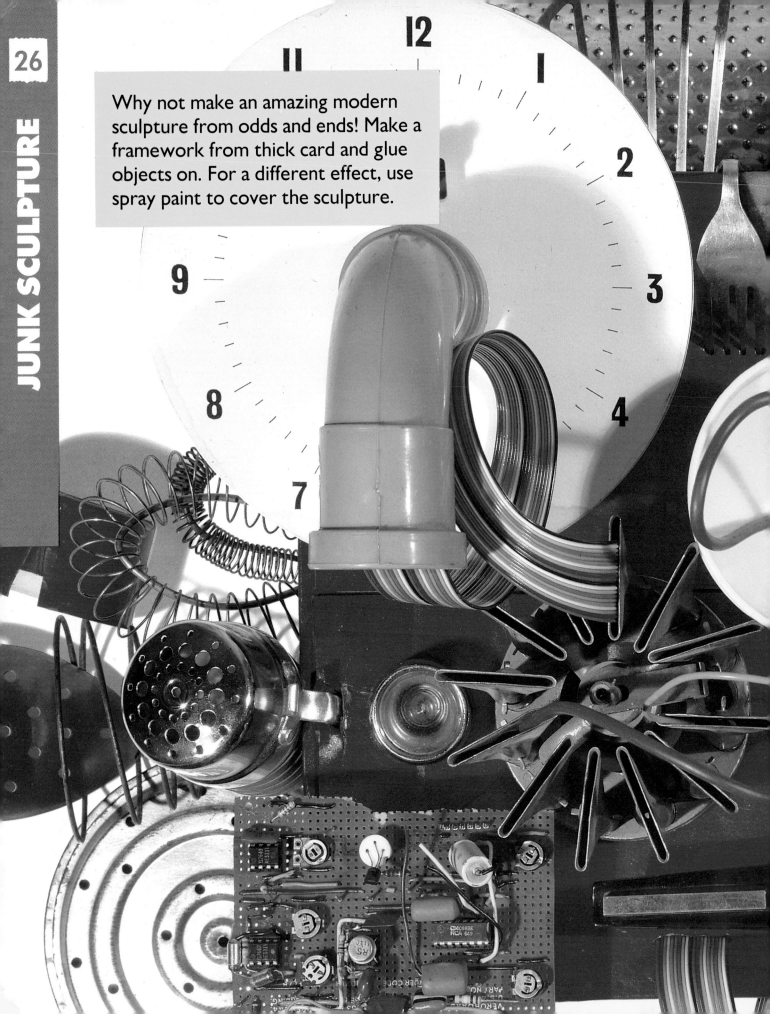

JUNK SCULPTURE

Why not make an amazing modern sculpture from odds and ends! Make a framework from thick card and glue objects on. For a different effect, use spray paint to cover the sculpture.

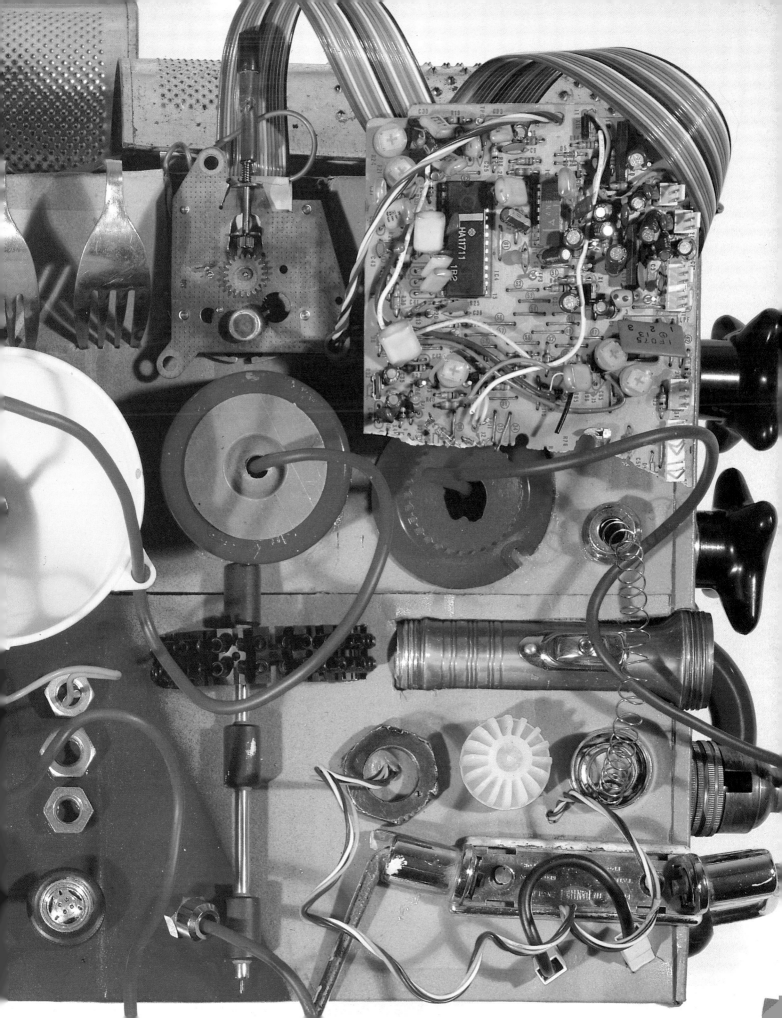

Cut a large hole in the side of a cardboard box. Look for bits and pieces to make a scene like our aquarium here. We used old plastic toys for the fish but you could also make your own from papier mâché or cardboard. Try making a model theatre in the same way with moving scenery and characters.

Here are some ideas for making bangles, badges and earrings from odds and ends. Look out for pieces of old jewellery that can be recycled, fabric scraps, buttons, beads and silver foil.

To make colourful bangles, use the inside section of a roll of sellotape or a piece cut from a plastic bottle. Cover the ring with fabric scraps or ribbons.

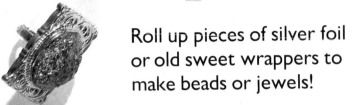

Roll up pieces of silver foil or old sweet wrappers to make beads or jewels!

Cover strips of card with fabric and glue on beads, buttons or small pieces of old jewellery to make badges. Tape a safety pin to the back of the badge.